# A FOCUSED PURSUIT
## IN CHINA

12/12/12

Mark,

awesome talking to you on
our way to NRT. I look
forward to reading
your book!

Regards,
Michael Meier
迈石无

# A FOCUSED PURSUIT IN CHINA

## 14 BUSINESS TIPS TO KNOW BEFORE YOU GO

MIKE MEIER, MBA

**Maximizer**
WORLD PUBLISHING
Hillsboro, Illinois USA

First Edition 2010
ISBN: 978-0-615-39117-5
Library of Congress Control Number: 2010933760

**Attention Corporations, Universities, Colleges,
and Professional Organizations:**
Quantity discounts are available on bulk purchases of this book
for educational, business, gift or sales promotion purposes,
or as premiums for increasing magazine subscriptions or
renewals. Special books or book excerpts may also be created
to fit specific needs. For more information, please contact:
Info@MaximizerWorld.com

*You can contact the author at:*
14ChinaTips@FOCUSEDPURSUIT.com

# CONTENTS

# CONTENTS

# ACKNOWLEDGMENTS

**Special Thanks to:**
Billy Lam, Amar B., Timothy Ferriss, Bi Jing,
Bruce K., Marge K., Stephen L., Dong Li, Christian L.,
Dean L., Sara N., Keith O., Chrissy S., Nancy T.,
Carrie W., James W., and Shanshan W.

**Extra Special Thanks to:**
Brenden, Kylie, Brady, Brian, Shannon, Josh,
Valerie, Rachel, Claire, Bruce, and Marge—
my muses from afar.

**Credits:**
Book Manufacturing: Thomson-Shore, Inc., Dexter,
    Michigan
Cover Design: Jennifer Spence, JenTrends Creative
    Works, Fort Worth, Texas
Editor: Jo-Ann Langseth, Warwick, Rhode Island
Editorial Insight: Tammy D. Bailey, DTM, Fort Worth,
    Texas & Steph McNelly, Lenexa, Kansas
Index: Martha Malnor, Malnor Indexing, Katy, Texas
Photos: Mike Meier, Billy Lam, and Korea Nazarene
    University
Interior Design & Typesetting: Julie Allred, BW&A
    Books, Inc., Durham, North Carolina

# FOREWORD

by China's Serial Entrepreneur
林贤斌 **BILLY LAM**,
Founder of AMR Audio,
Bdot Productions, and B-B Promo

Since you are reading this book, you know that **NOW is the time to do business in China!** You probably also know that business experiences may be completely different from what you're used to, whether you're from London or Los Angeles.

Although I'm Chinese by blood, I have always lived and worked around Westerners. I was born and raised in Hong Kong where I regularly assisted my family's company and its American and European customers. After studying in the States and working for a few multinational companies like IBM, I used my Western/Eastern hybrid business acumen to launch a series of profitable companies. I've done business throughout Europe, Australia, and India, **but there is no place I would rather be right now than China!**

For the past six years I've logged most of my time in Beijing, so I've seen many expatriates come and go. The ones who were sent home packing tried to apply their homespun business techniques and never connected with clients. For instance, I became friends with an information technology salesman from Miami. Even though his multinational firm supplied him with a large support staff of people trained to work in the Chinese business environment, he tried to do business his own way—and failed. After three months . . . six months . . . nine months . . . one year, he had no takers and went home unemployed.

You may have a brilliant idea, and you might be a smart person. But if you don't adhere to China's business culture and apply its tenets, you might also go home disappointed.

If you want to have a FOCUSED PURSUIT in China like Mike and me, then this book is a great starting point.

*A FOCUSED PURSUIT in China: 14 Business Tips to Know Before You Go* will definitely prepare you for the complicated road ahead. From networking to name cards, and from toasting to teamwork, Mike's tips are very insightful, especially coming from a *waìguórén* (foreigner). I'm a local, but Mike explains his principles in such a way that they should make complete sense when you personally face the situations discussed. By the time you apply the fourteen tips in China, you will be able to view China, as well as your home country, from a completely different perspective.

Enjoy your time in China, and good luck on your adventure ahead!

# ARE YOU
# **READY?**

Congratulations! In a matter of months, weeks, or days (let's hope not hours, minutes, or seconds), you will land in the People's Republic of China (PRC), ready to immerse yourself in an amazing business, personal, and cultural experience! With a population of more than 1.3 billion people, the country is becoming an increasingly dominant force in the world's economy (1).

*But . . . are you READY?*

According to the "2010 Global Relocation Trends Survey Report," published annually by Chicago-based Brookfield Global Relocation Services, doing successful business in China is no simple walk in the park (2). For the fourth consecutive year, China was found to be the most challenging foreign work destination for expatriates. On top of that, China led the list in foreign destination assignment failure.

*So, you still think you're READY?*

If you're reading this book, this may be your first

visit to China, or for that matter, anywhere in Asia, which is wonderful. I remember my first flight to Beijing. I was so nervous I couldn't even relax on the plane. I fidgeted for fourteen straight hours — all the way from Chicago!

However, before I left the States, I did my homework to prepare for the journey (as you are doing right now). Without the legwork, my initial experiences would have been shocking, rather than smooth.

Although you'll be surprised by how SIMILAR China is to other countries you may have visited, there are certainly jaw-dropping differences. *A FOCUSED PURSUIT in China: 14 Business Tips to Know Before You Go* is a concise, personally tested resource for you to use as you prepare for your upcoming opportunity. I've written this as if *we* were talking at a coffee shop, rather than *you* flipping through a lengthy encyclopedia.

Having grown up in between Chicago and St. Louis, the heartland of America, and having lived in the United States nearly all my life, I have an unapologetic American-based perspective. However, I have tried my best to make this book globally understandable by cutting out clichés, getting to the point, and providing clear examples. Hopefully, you'll "get it," whether you're from Albuquerque or Amsterdam.

The focus of my business and personal experience has been in my favorite Chinese city, Beijing. However, my network of friends and business associates from around the PRC concur that these observations and tips are relevant throughout the country, and even other parts of Southeast Asia.

If you ingrain the following pages into your brain, I promise you'll be much better informed and more prepared for your trip.

Now . . . are you READY??? Let your FOCUSED PURSUIT begin!

# CULTURE
# **SHOCKED!**

If you've ever traveled to a foreign country, you may have learned how to adapt to new surroundings, customs, and foods. If this is your first time out of the country, be prepared to get shocked—CULTURE SHOCKED!

In China:

- Most people DON'T speak English, ESPECIALLY cab drivers.
- You will be STARED AT because you are a foreigner, so get used to it.
- DOG MEAT is served at some relatively nice family restaurants.
- There are people literally EVERYWHERE!

Once you overcome these hurdles, you will continue to be so overloaded with stimuli that your brain won't know how to process it all! Unusual architecture will catch your eye, street vendors will try to sell you food you don't even remotely recognize, and gangs of bicyclists racing by at warp speed will almost give you a heart attack. Although you can only learn so much before you travel abroad, I recommend reading as much as possible about China and its culture. Empty out your local library's collection about Chinese history and culture. Solicit advice and borrow books from associates who have visited China. In these resources you will find topics not addressed in this book, including why not to buy a clock as a gift, how to "squat" efficiently, and why public restrooms have an interesting scent. Read *The 4-Hour Workweek* by Timothy Ferriss for a wealth of international travel tips (3). Print out related Wikipedia (4) entries, put them in a folder, and take them on the plane. Now that we have entered the digital age, you are welcome to keep our planet "green" by saving the documents on your netbook, iPad, or Kindle. Do everything and anything possible to prepare. (Above all, don't forget THIS book!)

When I visited China for the first time, a good friend of mine who was living in Beijing was able to ease me into various experiences. Without speaking a lick of the language, I was shown how to bargain with retailers, hail a cab, and judge the quality—and more important, the safety—of local establishments. Hopefully, when you arrive, you can utilize a go-to guy for the duration of your stay.

However, you are also welcome to use the fly-by-the-seat-of-your-pants method and just "take it all in" as it comes. Personally, I wasn't comfortable doing that, but if that's your travel preference, so be it, and more power to you. My Italian friend, Sara, who took Mandarin Chinese classes with me, preferred this method. She always jokingly said, "No matter what I experience, I will always be surprised!"

But did you know it may be more difficult adapting to your return from China than your arrival? The longer you stay in a foreign land, the more difficult it may be to transition back to your home country. This is called "reverse culture shock," and can become a very serious psychological condition. What was once familiar may become unfamiliar, which can be incredibly frustrating, or even clinically depressing.

My first return to the United States was quite unpleasant. Because I made it a priority to immerse myself in speaking Mandarin, I came back speaking a hybrid language: "Chinese English" or "Chinglish." My friends made fun of me or gave me strange looks because I spoke in sentences common to an eight-year-old and didn't even realize it. Also, because it's so cheap to eat well in Beijing, I never cooked. Because it was too expensive for me to eat out all the time when I arrived home, cooking on my own became an annoying chore. The intense, everyday stimulation of living in a foreign country made my small hometown seem dull and boring when I came back.

Fortunately, I made a full recovery. The Internet holds a vast array of resources, ranging from personal testimonies to tutorials presented by international departments at major universities (5). If you come back feeling the effects of reverse culture shock, take it seriously and ask for help.

On the other hand, you may enjoy your life, meet a beautiful man or woman, and decide to stay in China. When you write that book, I'll definitely read it!

# IT'S ALL ABOUT
# **THE "GUANGXI"**

Think of your top five clients . . .

How well do you REALLY know them?

Have you met their spouses? Have you ever sung karaoke with them? Can you remember having one too many beers together?

In China you might do all three—in the same night.

The foundation of all quality business dealings in the PRC is personal, connected relationships. The Chinese call it **"guangxi."** The more guangxi you possess, the farther you will go in business with your clients, and the more likely that they will refer you to their friends. The less guangxi you have, the more likely you may have to resign yourself to returning to your home country early, empty handed, and disappointed.

I'm not Chinese, so it's hard for me to explain guangxi and its importance as a local could. It's like rapport, but not really. It's an intangible, but you have to obtain it. You can go looking for it, but you may not find it. Then again, you may not look for it and have it appear in your lap.

For instance, I hit it off with a woman at a networking function in Beijing. I gave her my full attention, asked intelligent questions, and answered all her questions. Well, I don't know what she saw in me, but I became her new best friend! In a matter of months, she shared with me great insight about Chinese business culture, introduced me to several of her colleagues through various luncheons at her company, and brought me to amazing networking gatherings. I was chauffeured to events at places ranging from luxurious hotels to hole-in-the-wall crevices that even my GPS would have trouble finding!

The Chinese are loyal. When you cultivate strong friendships in China, you may make friendships that will last a lifetime. On personal, emotional, and professional levels, you can't go wrong. Do your best to develop sincere, long-lasting relationships, and in addition to increasing your business prospects, you will greatly enjoy your life on the other side of the world.

# UPSIDE-DOWN
# **MEETING FORMAT**

Unless you were prepped before you left, your first few business meetings may be a bit confusing. No, strike that—headache-giving, brain-freezing, speechlessly confusing.

Using an American model, which is most likely generalized from a Western perspective, the first meeting with a client is almost like a sprint to spending. You both have done your homework and understand, at least for the most part, how each of you can help the other. The in-person meeting is the time to "get things done."

If there happens to be a second meeting, it will simply finish up the details that weren't addressed in the first meeting, celebrate the finalizing of a contract, and explain the transition of the transaction. You then have dinner at a nice restaurant while displaying your best manners, hoping you don't do anything stupid or crude to screw up the deal you just inked.

If this is your general expectation, you may be in for a surprise. First of all, try not to think that YOUR way of doing meetings is the ONLY way. The Chinese beg to differ on the meaning of "absolute truth" on this matter.

In China, the initial meeting with a new client may very well be the first time you've met him or her. It could be that you were referred by a client, or didn't really talk beforehand and then set up a formal meeting. You may have a general idea of their field and what they want to discuss, but you didn't get into details over the phone.

The first meeting is almost like a blind date— getting to know a person, not giving too much information, and trying to make them think that yours is the best company they will ever do business with. You talk about the enduring legacy of your company, your vision for the future, and how your company and their company could work together on amazing projects down the road. Then you have a three-hour lunch, eat more than you thought possible, and REALLY get to know your client.

One of my first business meetings just a week after I arrived in China was absolutely surreal. My team had eight people on our side of the table, and our newly-acquainted business partner had eight people on his side of the table. Only the presidents from each side actually talked during the meeting, giving introductions about their respective companies and the teams they were honored to lead. The other fourteen of us were just for show—similar to the Mercedes-Benz we drove to the meeting. (It was rented for the day, but made a great first impression!)

The luncheon was unbelievable. I thought we had walked into an aquarium, but it was actually a restaurant where you handpick the fish you want to end up on your plate. Lunch had to have lasted three hours—talking and eating, talking and drinking, and more talking, eating, and drinking. When lunch was over, it was so late in the day that it was pointless to go back to the office.

The second meeting was when we really started creating plans, making proposals, and setting deadlines. But without the first meeting and the lunch—all developing the guangxi—the second meeting would NEVER have happened.

When you find yourself in those new and exciting types of business meetings, relish the experiences, analyze the situations, and enjoy your time away from the office!

# NAME CARD

## 101

Ever heard of a "name card?" I hadn't either, until about two weeks before my first trip to China. I was on my way to the Super Bowl and coincidentally sat next to a Chinese woman on the plane. Even more serendipitous, she lived in Beijing and worked as an executive for General Electric (GE). At the end of the flight, she turned to me and said, "Here is my name card." Clueless, I took the card, looked at her, looked at the card, blinked a few times, and realized what she had given me.

"Name card" is the Eastern term for "business card." (The joke was on me!)

Why do they call it a "name card?" I don't know for certain. Maybe it goes back to the whole guangxi aspect of putting the person before the business. Or maybe it's because many people in China who don't have businesses still have cards.

Because of the language barrier, your English-only

cards will not work well for you in China. Make some special name cards for your trip, or have them printed for a quarter of the price when you arrive. Since English is the unofficial second language in China and is considered by many to be the universal language of commerce, one side of your card should be in English, and the other side should be in simplified Chinese characters. If you have space, put the characters above the English words and leave the other side blank. Many of your clients, especially if they are older, simply can't read or speak English, so don't punish them for that. You're there to do business, not lecture them on the importance of speaking English as a member of the global village.

In the United States, when you have an initial business conversation with someone, you usually strike up an exchange and then casually hand over your card when your chat comes to a close. Or if you're really selective, you don't give them a card at all, unless you see yourself doing business together, or referring them to others.

In the PRC, the FIRST step in a conversation is the exchange of name cards. It really makes sense when you think about it. If you obtain someone's card, you will more quickly learn the name of the person's company, position or title within the company, and where the company is based. Reference to the card streamlines the first five minutes of the conversation, when normally you would have to ask and answer the same basic questions before really getting to know the person. This practice also goes for large-table business meetings — you hand everyone in the room your name card before the meeting even begins, and get their name cards in return. Then you can line them up on the table in front of you, in the order in which your business partners are sitting.

Oh, and the PRESENTATION of the name card exchange is key. When you hand someone your card, hold it facing your new business associate with both your thumbs and index fingers; that way the card can easily be read from the beginning. Your business associate will receive the handoff in a quite gentle, caring manner, with their fingers mirroring yours. Vice versa ensues when you receive his card. After that, it is very common to study the card intently, compliment them on how important they are based on their title and company, and make some outlandish statement about how you could do business together. You're probably thinking I'm kidding, right? But just wait — you'll see!

# THE TOAST
## (NOT THE BREAD KIND)

When I think back to the many toasts I presented, received, or observed in China, I internally chuckle and outwardly smile at this fun-loving custom.

From my experiences, toasting at parties, banquets, and dinner meetings is more common than it is in the United States. Special shot glasses are even set aside to perform the toasts, no matter what alcoholic beverage is involved.

Most of the upscale dinners I attended with clients featured large, round tables with a rotating circular glass mount in the middle to serve the food. (Some in the U.S. call it a "lazy Susan." I feel sorry for Susan, wherever she is!) While at dinners like these, two types of toasts occur: public and private. Most of the initial, public toasts are directed at specific individuals, acknowledging them for their leadership and hopes for future business. After the person toasting stands and presents the toast (holding a special toast glass), everyone at the table, including the recipient of the toast, also stands and raises their glasses. Once the words of appreciation have been spoken, the two individuals of the toast down their drinks, followed by the rest of the audience. Then everyone sits down, fills their shot glasses again, and prepares for the next toasts. Don't look surprised or act annoyed if you have to repeat this custom twenty times over the next sixty minutes. It happens to the best of us.

I remember one of my first toasts when I couldn't speak or understand any Mandarin. Sitting with a table of fifteen or more, an elderly gentleman across the table from me presented a toast. Moments later, my Chinese colleagues informed me that he was addressing the toast to me! He barely made out my name, delivering the toast completely in Chinese, but everyone was so caught up in the moment (or so inebriated) that no one translated for me. I just smiled, gladly accepted the toast, and drank up. (Later, come to think of it, I even forgot to ask what the toast was about!)

If you keep your eyes peeled, you'll see that once the two principals involved in the public toast finish off their drinks, they present their empty glasses to each other, showcasing the inside bottom of the glass. I assume this says, "Look inside! There's nothing left because I fully take in our relationship!"

As the marathon dinner continues, and people start loosening up from the drinks and the food, you may have specific individuals come to your seat to offer a private toast. Instead of making a big show, it is just for the two of you. Again, you stand, raise your glass, and wait for them to explain their toast. And then, as you hit glasses . . .

WAIT! Don't hit his glass just yet!

When clinking glasses, it is customary to hit the lowest part of your comrade's glass. This is a sign of respect and understanding of the culture. It can also become a fun game of "How Low Can You Go?" With luck and focused attention, it will not become an air toast. After you drink, show the inner bottom of the glass and take your seat.

Some of my favorite memories in China were born at the dinner table. Thank you, Susan.

chapter
**6**

# BEWARE OF
# **BÁIJIǓ**

After reading an entire chapter on toasting, you may be thinking, *"Wow! Do they really drink THAT much at business meetings in China?"* I don't want to stereotype the Chinese as lushes, but yes, they do like their liquor. On top of that, many of them have a VERY low tolerance. Several mini shots of beer can add up quickly!

Why do they drink so much? I think it goes back to the guangxi. By getting intoxicated with someone, you are showing mutual respect in your willingness to let loose and trust them enough to let your guard down. You will be able to see how your client acts when he is buzzed or drunk, and vice versa. Some have made the claim to me that if you don't drink, you'll never garner successful business in Chengdu, Chongqing, or whatever Chinese city you visit.

That could be the case, but if you have strong moral concerns or physical reasons for not drinking, stick to them. You may be respecting a more important

God than the "Almighty Renminbi." You could tell your guests that you are allergic to alcohol, or that your religious beliefs simply forbid it. You may be surprised— *Zhōngguóréns* (Chinese citizens) seem to be very accepting and intrigued by differing cultures and beliefs.

But not drinking alcohol should not hinder you from toasting. Apple juice and sparkling ciders both look enough like beer to not have your drink choice questioned. Sparkling water, 7-Up, and Sprite can also resemble alcoholic drinks, and obviously have much less kick. Just ask the waiter for one of these alternatives so you can toast with others. When everyone else has already had one too many, the last question they'll ask is "what are you drinking?"

If you end up toasting with báijiǔ (whiskey) instead of píjiǔ (beer), be aware that it is VERY strong, even if you normally throw back alcohol like water. Know your maximum tolerance level and have someone keep you accountable if needed. Although you most likely won't be driving, the Chinese government is very serious about catching drunk drivers, so don't even think about risking it. Besides, cab service is extremely cheap. In Beijing you can be taxied across the entire 17.4-million-person city for less than 100 RMB ($15 USD) (6).

chapter
**7**

# "HEY, WATCH
**YOUR MOUTH!"**

Traveling abroad for the first time is a life-changing experience. For me, it was one of the most nerve-wracking decisions I'd ever made. But my experiences in China, as well as in Europe and other parts of Asia, help me see the world through a larger, clearer lens. I understand better now how the United States is viewed around the world, and because of that, I've been able to create business opportunities I could never have fathomed.

However, you still need to be careful in China, whether alone or in a group. Traveling to a foreign country almost immediately translates to being responsible for understanding and complying with foreign customs, foreign laws, and foreign enforcement of those laws. Simply put, one slip of the tongue could strongly offend someone, lose your company's account, or possibly get you arrested or deported.

My best advice is to do more listening than talking.

If you tell your new business contact that you know just about everything there is to know about China, you will come off as arrogant and disrespectful of the culture. Therefore, even if you've done your homework and have a good feel for certain situations, it is many times better to act as if everything is a new experience. You won't offend anyone because they assume that you don't know anything! Additionally, I've found the Chinese enjoy orienting new people to their traditions because they are proud of them. Many customs have been passed down for generations and are thousands of years old. China, of all places, knows the meaning of "old." According to a 2009 study done in conjunction with China's State Administration of Cultural Heritage and State Bureau of Surveying and Mapping, the Great Wall is 5,500 miles long (8,851 km) and 2,500 years old (7). The "toddler" United States of America, by comparison, is still baby-stepping its way toward its 250th birthday!

The People's Republic of China is a Communist country, meaning that freedom of speech is not a simple right as in most democratic nations. Learn to keep your comments "politically correct."

When I visited Beijing at the beginning of 2009, I quickly found that "Obama Mania" had spread to the Far East. While many people were in awe of the new

American president's public speaking abilities, others were wary of the new man in office.

"So what do you think of Obama?" a local Chinese company executive asked me over dinner.

I simply replied, "He is our leader, and I respect him." Regardless of my own personal opinion of the President, I came off as neither a strong supporter nor adamant opponent.

Maybe it was just a common question because President Obama's campaign and election results were known throughout the world. Or maybe it was a question posed to judge my character. If I'd admitted any kind of disdain for him, or even a reservation, would I also criticize other superiors, including those at my new workplace?

Shy away from talking about the Chinese government in particular. The Communist Party is the only accepted party, so there is no room for dissent. While walking alone in the Forbidden City, having dinner with new business associates, or anywhere in between, if you succumb to a sudden urge to disparage President Hu Jintao regarding ill treatment of those living in Tibet, condemn "Chairman Mao" for torturing his own people, or even mention Tian'anmen Square and June 4, 1989, in the same sentence, be ready for a rude awakening. It is the responsibility of party members (by whom you could be completely surrounded at the time) to report you to the authorities. Such comments could brand you a political dissident, an activist, or a spy.

If in fact you are detained, the Public Security Bureau (PSB) will not read you your rights—because you don't really have that many while in their custody (8). If you think they'll let you make a phone call for help from your country's local embassy, don't count on it. After a few hours of interrogation, they may require you to buy a plane ticket and leave the country immediately. (Officially, the authorities can only detain you for seventy-two hours before they are required to contact your country's embassy (9).)

Americans already get a bad rap for being loud, boisterous tourists in other countries, so don't fuel this opinion. Simply be mindful of your words and conduct yourself in a professional manner, and no problems will come your way.

chapter
8

# WHAT IS POWER?

*Don't Know Much About American History* is an audio book I bought at the beginning of a road-trip vacation through the Rocky Mountains (10). It contained a story about former U.S. Federal Bureau of Investigation (FBI) Director J. Edgar Hoover. Hoover maintained records on more than 80,000 people whom the United States government considered "suspicious." Because only he had access to this highly sensitive information, many of his critics claim he kept his job for so long because he had dirt on so many people— especially those working around him.

It won't be your resume, sense of humor, or ravishing good looks that help you keep your job, rise through the ranks, or find new business in China.

Information is power.

To put this in perspective, I remember one particular job in China that was extremely difficult for me. It wasn't because the work was hard, but rather because my employer gave me little to no information about the assignments I was expected to complete.

One Monday morning, just a few minutes after I booted up my computer, checked my email, and settled in for the day, my boss approached my desk.

"Mike, we will be leaving for a meeting in five minutes. Get ready."

I knew nothing of the meeting or whom it was with, but I went along as instructed.

The meeting with the Beijing-based firm was completely in Mandarin. I could not keep up, nor could my translator, so I had absolutely no idea what was being discussed. During a quick intermission, my boss came to me again.

"Mike, do you have an extra I.D. photo with you?"

Interestingly enough, since I had just taken a photo for my new work I.D. card, I had an extra in my wallet, so I handed it off to him. I was still puzzled, but didn't see any harm in his motives.

After the break, the meeting resumed. Soon after, a photographer was brought in, and I was motioned to the front of the room. They handed me a beautiful certificate (with my I.D. photo as the centerpiece), and I posed for a photo with our partner's CEO.

So my boss wouldn't lose face, I didn't question the picture at the time, but rather asked my interpreter what the photo was all about.

"They are celebrating the fact that you will be working with them in the near future."

Again, my boss came to me with one final request. I had finally caught on that something wasn't right.

"Mike, do you have your passport with you?"

"Why do you need my passport?" I enquired.

"They need a copy of it."

"And why do they need a copy of my passport?" I winced even more.

"Because they are applying you for a Saudi Arabia visa."

"WHAT???"

Since I had no desire to leave China at the time, I was later able to put the kibosh on his plan. But because my boss had all the information about that day's events, he was in control and was able to wield his power over me.

Here is some advice to keep you away from situations where a lack of information could get you in trouble, or keep you from being successful in business in China.

**#1: Don't volunteer too much information.** Unless your boss or co-workers absolutely need information about your personal life or previous work experiences to complete some type of work task, don't give it to them. Always ask yourself, "Why do they want or need this information?" It could be that they truly need the information, have ulterior motives, or are asking an indirect question related to something else. But the more information you give out, the less power and control you have in the business environment.

People in China simply don't volunteer information. If you ask a specific question, you will receive a specific answer. Employers and prospective customers will give you just enough information so that you might not ask any more questions. Don't take offense: they are only protecting themselves.

**#2: Answer a question with a question.** This is a fun improvisational comedy game, too, but in this case, it is a great way to re-direct the attention away from you. You may be asked by a prospective customer, "Do you work with other Chinese companies?" If you want to keep your client list secretive (or you simply don't have many clients), you can respond by saying, "Do you prefer working with companies that have a more global variety of customers?"

**#3: Ask questions, but not too many questions.** Sometimes your question asking could get on your boss's nerves or slightly annoy a new client. He may ask, "Why are you asking so many questions?" The best way to respond is to play dumb. As long as the occasion suits it, you can simply reply, "I've only been here for ___ months and am just trying to understand the culture better." Most Chinese understand how different their culture is from other countries, so they will likely understand your response. Any questions?

chapter
9

# THERE'S NO "I"
## IN TEAM

The Western version of the corporate ladder is a pissing contest of individual merits. Agreed? Darwin's "Survival of the Fittest" is the epitome of this dynamic. Working more hours, garnering more clients, and selling more product should move you quickly to the top of the company.

Sorry, but this doesn't apply in Tianjin, Shenyang, or even Nanjing.

For example, when I started working at a new company, my laptop was not linked to our office's copier/printer. My work required major amounts of printing on a regular basis, so obviously I needed that basic freedom. In a department with five Chinese all in their early twenties, only two spoke solid English. Although I didn't understand a word they were saying, the minute I announced to the room that I couldn't print and wondered if there was a wireless connection, my entire team sprang into action. One person inspected my computer, another found the software to install the printer, and another found me a network cable. Within a few moments, my problem was solved.

The PRC business culture is mostly composed of team players, not individualists who seek status and promotions for themselves. It is their nature to labor in synergy. While Westerners tend to pile responsibilities, problems, and projects onto themselves to impress management, the Chinese work together.

At your workplace, do you always eat with your coworkers? Or do you eat alone? While on a job in northern China, it seemed to me that my coworkers always ate out together. My teammates took me under their wing, showed me great restaurants within walking distance, and gave me names for the foods they enjoyed placing in front of me. (Seaweed was my first adventure; it wasn't a pleasant one.) It's not that they felt sorry for me. They just naturally tended to be there for each other—even for lunch.

# READING BETWEEN
# **THE LINES**

On a scale of 1 to 10, how good of a liar are you? After forgetting about a meeting or project deadline, have you ever told a tiny, but sort-of-true white lie about why you didn't come through? Did your lie actually work?

If so, in *Zhōngguó* (China), you'll be among like-minded people.

No, I'm not implying that the Chinese are patho-logical liars. But a culture of indirect communication exists, much of which is full of simple, seemingly harmless white lies. In fact, it is actually considered MORE respectful to lie than to be direct and tell the truth. It is a sign of respect.

After an extended night of pampering at my favor-ite sauna, I woke up an hour late for work. When my boss asked me where I'd been that morning, I told him I must have gotten food poisoning because I had spent my entire morning clearing my bowels in the bathroom. (At the time, my words were much more colorful and convincing!)

With a smile on his face, a short chuckle, and a glint in his eye, he replied, "Okay. Well, I know it's hard getting used to the food here. Get to work."

Another example of indirect communication comes up when your boss asks when your project is going to be finished. Translation? *The project was due YESTER-DAY, so get it on my desk as soon as possible.*

Indirect communication also applies to other types of relationships. As a single guy, I've experienced countless ways that girls turn down dates, including "Let's just be friends," "I have another commitment," and "I have a friend in town." The Chinese (both male and female) have perfected this craft. Learn to be sensitive, and pick up on cues when your invitations are turned down.

On the other hand, if someone is VERY direct with you, they are probably telling you the truth. Have you ever tried to lie while yelling or screaming at someone? As a student of communication, I know that verbal and nonverbal communication usually mirror each other. Therefore, pay close attention to your colleagues and learn to read how the people around you communicate, but don't get a brain blister doing it (11).

# "NO—
# AFTER YOU!"

I miss China. One of my first impressions, which holds true to this day, is that the Chinese are EXTREMELY polite. Americans are respectful for the most part, but we usually don't go above and beyond the call of duty. Upon my initial arrival in China, I found that people opened doors for me, let me onto the elevator and through doors first, and even poured my drinks. I was definitely skeptical at first, but was hardly going to turn down the royal treatment.

Initially, I thought my new acquaintances and business associates were being especially friendly to me because I was a *lǎowài* (foreigner). One of my cultural mentors was an American who has lived in Beijing for the past six years and is married to a native Beijinger. He advised me to be VERY careful in everything I did and everywhere I went, and to remember that this was NOT the United States. He gave me a few reasons why it would be completely normal for the Chinese to treat me exorbitantly well.

"One, Mike, is that you're a well-dressed guy doing business in China. Because of that, they naturally assume that you're very rich. If there is even a remote possibility that you're loaded, people will be much nicer to you because they will want you to put money their way.

"Two, you have 'Green Card' pasted on your forehead. You may not see it, but many cute Chinese girls would love to serve your every need, on the off chance that you will take them home with you. I mean, not to your apartment in town, but your apartment a continent away."

This "food for thought" was definitely consumed. However, I did find out that along with businesspeople and beautiful women being overly helpful, there is a cultural norm to at least present oneself as humble and serving. I began to pay more attention to my day-to-day situations, played the "game" of unrelenting, requited "niceness," and expediently earned the respect of colleagues, friends, and new acquaintances.

When leaving a building or room, be courteous and let people go ahead of you. If someone says, "No—you first," with a smile, simply and firmly reply, "No—YOU first!" It could quickly become a game of back-and-forth until you're both smiling. The same concept applies to entering an elevator.

At a dinner setting, someone might offer you the most important seat. Again, casually let him know that you want *him* to sit there, until it reaches the point of, "Well, if you insist, okay." Not long after, the bottled drinks or teapots may arrive. (Drinking cold tap water is not recommended and it's rarely served, as the water in China is not known for its sparkling cleanliness.) The person next to you may offer to pour your drink. Playfully try to steal the container from him or her, attempting to give them the honor of your pouring their drink. The never-ending "after you" game happily continues.

I can recall countless situations when this happened, and I laughed wholeheartedly with the person on the other side of the exchange. It was an easy icebreaker, which led to some great, meaningful conversation.

Interestingly enough, I subconsciously brought this new habit back with me to the U.S. (I also still have a habit of exchanging "name cards" with two hands!) I have always been polite, but my friends and family thought I had taken it to a completely new level. It seems I had to go to the other side of the globe for people to notice that I am actually very courteous. (Better late than never.)

chapter
**12**

# BECOME A
# "VERY IMPORTANT PANDA"

Busy people are important people, at least in the eyes of the Chinese. Along with being humble, letting it be known that you are always busy can go a long way in laying the foundation for future business relationships.

I learned this concept at a dinner function, where many of the top accountants in Asia were being recognized. After I'd explained my job in great detail to one of the honorees, he replied, "You must be VERY busy! You're a V.I.P. Do you know what that means?"

"Maybe," I replied. "What does it mean here in China?"

"It means Very Important Panda!"

When I kept my eyes open in the community, I spotted many lurking "pandas."

One time, just before a flight to Hong Kong, a severe pain in my back was annoying me to no end. Luckily, I found a massage shop right inside the airport terminal. I walked into the shop and saw the strangest sight—a man talking LOUDLY on his cell phone, while simultaneously getting a neck massage! After picking up on their conversations, I could perceive that everyone in the room sensed the man was very important.

Fortunately, he wasn't the funniest *xióngmāo* (panda) I spotted. Late one Friday night, I journeyed to my favorite sauna for some rest and relaxation. To give you some background, Chinese "saunas" also many times include opportunities for foot and back massages, luxurious buffets, and Las Vegas-style shows. They use the word "sauna," but it actually translates more closely to the Western idea of a spa. My favorite sauna had a large, heated pool, seven different whirlpools with temperatures ranging from freezing to volcanic, steam rooms, and countless showers. Although they provide you with pajama-like clothes after you finish the water-based activities, prior to that, everyone saunters around completely naked. So leave your swimming trunks (and self-consciousness) at home!

While at the sauna, I was escorted for a foot massage to a large open room with stadium-like seating. As dozens watched the lone foreigner being seated, I was placed next to a Chinese man probably around fifty years old.

He wasn't alone.

With a cigarette in one hand and a beer in the other, the man rattled away at a conversation on his Bluetooth headset. He was flanked by two beautiful women, one massaging his feet and legs, and the other massaging his neck and head. Everyone in the room (including me) wanted this guy's name card! Who was he—China's version of Donald Trump? He ended up receiving a stack of business cards, and all he did was get a massage. I definitely learned from a professional "panda."

chapter
**13**

# LEARN THE LANGUAGE—
## SHÌ ZHĒN DE

I absolutely LOVE talking and writing about my experiences in China. One of the reasons I was introduced to so many interesting experiences is because I learned the national language—Mandarin Chinese.

*But Mike—isn't Chinese difficult to learn?*

English was hard for me to learn at one point, too, but I got through it. Although that is an overgeneralization, in just a short amount of time you can pick up enough spoken Chinese to feel comfortable meeting new people, directing a cab, and ordering food.

A month after arriving in China, I worked with a private tutor three days a week, two hours a day, for three months. Instead of learning how to speak, write, and read Mandarin, I focused only on the speaking part. (My Western friends in China who are learning to read claim that you have to know 2,000 characters to read a newspaper.) *Pīnyīn* is the English phonetic version of Chinese. You can learn Chinese words, phrases, and greetings in no time without having to mess with Chinese characters. Just like learning any new skill or language, the more effort you put forth, the greater results you will gain.

*But Mike, seriously, do I have to learn the language?*

No, not necessarily. But if you want to get the most out of your time in China, go for it. Believe me—it pays off. Besides, more and more Americans now going to China for business can already speak the language. According to "Chinese: An Expanding Field," a report on the progress of Chinese language instruction in American schools, nearly 52,000 high school students are currently learning the language, and nearly 800 colleges have the Chinese language in their curricula (12).

Along with working in China, I was also involved locally with Toastmasters International (13). District 85 needed an additional speaker for its national conference, so I presented a brief seminar on speech-crafting (14). Although 99% of my audience was Chinese, my seminar and handouts were in English. As an icebreaker, I gave my entire introduction in Mandarin. The audience interrupted with heavy gasps and long laughter! They couldn't believe I had learned their language so quickly. I grabbed their attention from the beginning, held on to it throughout the lecture, and made some new friends and contacts soon after that.

I also played a lot of *pingpangqiú* (ping-pong/table tennis) in China, the country's national sport. As a USA Table Tennis (USATT) lifetime member and International Table Tennis Federation (ITTF) White Badge Umpire, it is safe to say I immensely enjoy the sport. One weekend I traveled to the city of Hohhot, located in Inner Mongolia province. The city hosted a national event that featured many of the world's top table tennis players, since the best of the best are from China. Out of roughly 500 spectators sitting in the bleachers, I was the only foreigner. However, because I spoke *pǔtōng huà* (Mandarin), I made many friends at the event. One of them was a sports executive from a nearby province, who invited me to dinner that night at one of the city's finest restaurants. Little did I know that twenty other guests were invited, including several of the provincial coaches busy earlier at the tournament. They welcomed my presence with open arms.

Although my Chinese teacher offered to give me lessons via Skype upon returning to the States, I instead purchased the Rosetta Stone language-learning software, which has kept my spoken Chinese at a relatively high level (15).

Without learning to speak Chinese, I doubt I would have enjoyed my time there as much, or even written this book — *shì zhēn de*. (Seriously.)

# UNLUCKY
## #13

Along with the number 4, the number 13 is unlucky in China. Therefore, for culture's sake, I couldn't finish this book with 13 chapters! The lucky number in China is 8, so be on the lookout for 8's on price tags for items in stores in China. It is a great marketing tactic.

I'm gratified that you have come this far with me. By now, you should have picked up some solid, practical advice for your time in China. Now you know how to present a business card, give a toast, and even spot a panda!

The business potential of the country is unfathomable. Major cities like Shanghai, Shenzhen, and Shenyang are very modern compared to places like London, Los Angeles, and Luxembourg. However, China's economic expansion and strong capitalist mindset have only been active since 1979. With the enhanced availability of the Internet, video conferencing, and mobile technology, large companies and corporations can ill afford to ignore global expansion, especially into China. Although the World Wide Web is opening up more opportunity for business relationships, having in-person relationships is more important than ever. Because of that, the number of direct flights to China is increasing every day. No matter where you live in the world, you will be able to travel to China quickly and smoothly, especially compared to a few years ago. If you stick with one airline for your trips, those frequent flier miles will add up enough for a free trip back to your country. Maybe by then you'll be able to go more for pleasure than business!

With world business, political, and social environments perpetually changing, *A FOCUSED PURSUIT in China: 14 Business Tips to Know Before You Go* will always be a work in progress. I encourage you to visit http://www.FOCUSEDPURSUIT.com to post your stories from abroad, give me feedback about this book, or encourage me to consider other topics to cover in future editions. You can always email me directly at 14ChinaTips@FOCUSEDPURSUIT.com.

*Màn zǒu hé zài jiàn*! (Be safe and good-bye!)

# EPILOGUE

It is a joy to write about my business experiences in China. In the future I hope to write more about my extensive travels, cultural encounters, and unfortunate incidents. I am also excited to travel anywhere in the world to speak to groups on this topic, whether it is to 50 or 5,000. If you or your organization would like me to come and speak about Chinese business culture, train your employees, or lead a seminar at your next event, or if you have any questions, comments, or suggestions, feel free to email me at 14ChinaTips@ FOCUSEDPURSUIT.com.

Thanks again for reading *A FOCUSED PURSUIT in China: 14 Business Tips to Know Before You Go*. If you found this book helpful and would like someone else to read it, you can purchase additional copies at http:// www.FOCUSEDPURSUIT.com.

# NOTES

1. United Nations Populations Division. "World Population Prospects: The 2008 Revision Population Database." http://esa.un.org/unpp.
2. Brookfield Global Relocation Services. "2010 Global Relocation Trends Survey Report." http://www.brookfieldgrs.com.
3. Ferriss, Timothy. *The 4-Hour Workweek: Escape 9-5, Live Anywhere, and Join the New Rich.* New York: Crown Publishers, 2007.
4. "China." http://en.wikipedia.org/China.
5. "As American as Fish and Chips: A guide for students returning from studying abroad." http://educationabroad.bgsu.edu/pdfs/Re-entry%20Handbook.pdf.
6. "Beijing Population Exceeds 17.4 Million." China.org by Yang Xi. 12/04/07. http://www.china.org.cn/english/China/234343.htm.
7. "Great Wall of China 'even longer.'" 20 Apr. 2009. http://news.bbc.co.uk/2/hi/asia-pacific/8008108.stm.
8. Visit http://travel.state.gov to register your trip and let your embassy know you are there in case you go missing. You can also sign up for regular travel warning updates. The website also has great information regarding cultural explanations.

9. Personal correspondence—U.S. Department of State, 07/10/09.

10. Davis, Kenneth C. *Don't Know Much About American History*. New York: HarperCollins Audio, 1995.

11. "Brain blister" is a term I first came upon in American tennis star Andre Agassi's memoir. (Agassi, Andre. *Open: An Autobiography*. New York: Knopf Doubleday Publishing Group, 2009.) A brain blister is what his father trained him to give to his opponents. Although Andre's life doesn't have much to do with Chinese business culture, this is the most public way I could think of for plugging his book and thanking him for being a sports role model for me while growing up. Andre, if you ever read this, thank you!

12. Reavy, Amanda. "Springfield, Chatham schools consider offering online Mandarin Chinese courses." *The State Journal-Register*. 28 Dec. 2009.

13. Toastmasters International. http://www.Toastmasters.org.

14. District 85 Toastmasters. http://www.ChinaToastmasters.org.

15. Rosetta Stone. http://www.RosettaStone.com.

# INDEX

# ABOUT THE AUTHOR

**Mike Meier, MBA**, is Managing Director of FOCUSED PURSUIT LLC. Mike earned his MBA from Texas Wesleyan University in Fort Worth. He graduated magna cum laude with a bachelor's degree in mass communication from Olivet Nazarene University near Chicago, Illinois. Mike is a Distinguished Toastmaster (DTM) and has given presentations, lectures, and seminars in China, Taiwan, and the Republic of Korea, as well as throughout the United States and Canada.

When he is not writing or speaking, Mike loves to travel. He has visited nearly 20 countries, speaks Mandarin Chinese, Korean, and Spanish, and is always looking to earn more frequent-flier miles. Mike is an International Table Tennis Federation (ITTF) White Badge Umpire, which provides him the opportunity to officiate professional table tennis tournaments worldwide. Currently, Mike teaches international business management at Korea Nazarene University near Seoul, but Hillsboro, Illinois, will always be home.

You can email Mike at
14ChinaTips@FOCUSEDPURSUIT.com
and follow him on Twitter @FOCUSEDPURSUIT

# ABOUT FOCUSED PURSUIT

FOCUSED PURSUIT LLC is dedicated to "helping clients achieve their personal and professional goals." The company provides leadership training for groups ranging from small businesses to Fortune 100 companies. FOCUSED PURSUIT is also one of 230 worldwide affiliates of The Highlands Company, publisher of the Highlands Ability Battery, the gold standard among assessment tools measuring individual abilities. You can learn more about FOCUSED PURSUIT at http://www.FOCUSEDPURSUIT.com.